ADOBE PHOTOSHOP ELEMENTS USER GUIDE 2024

A fascinating Guide with all the nitty-gritty for Effective Usage

Zion Peace

Table of Contents

INTRODUCTION

"Match color and tone" is one of the new capabilities in Photoshop Elements 2024. Users can choose from predefined colors and tones or use their own photographs for this. Adobe says, "Click once, and then adjust brightness, saturation, and hue."

Users may create a reel of photographs they like with text, graphics, and effects with the new Photo Reels feature. Users may export them as GIFs or MP4s, making it simple and quick to share them on a variety of social networking networks.

Photoshop Elements 2024 now has access to the choose topic capabilities that are widely used in Adobe Lightroom, Adobe Camera Raw, and Photoshop, thanks to Adobe AI. Users can choose the subject of an image or merely the background with ease thanks to automatic choices, which facilitates localized editing and compositing.

Popular one-click image altering options are now available through a Quick Actions menu. One-click changes, for instance, can be used to colorize images, smooth skin, remove or blur backgrounds, and much more. This menu now includes an AI-powered "JPEG Artifacts Removal" option that automatically enhances and smoothes compressed JPEG photos.

The Guided Edits feature of both Photoshop and Premiere Elements are well-known. With the aid of these detailed lessons, users may successfully complete projects and common editing tasks. There are currently 62 of these tutorials in Photoshop Elements 2024, featuring new ones for Amazing Landscape and Replace Background.

Photoshop Elements 2024 has a completely redesigned user interface in addition to these additional features. The app's fonts, icons, buttons, and colors have all been updated by Adobe, and users now have the choice to choose between bright and dark settings.

A redesigned user interface, additional Guided Edits, matching color and tone, and a few more enhancements bring the total number of new features and improvements in Adobe Premiere Elements 2024 to 26. Photoshop Elements 2024 has similar changes and new capabilities.

With AI-automated Highlight Reels, the latest version of Premiere Elements also partakes in the "Reels" experience. This feature, which emphasizes and includes excellent motion and close-up video, promises to produce engaging video compilations.

To further enhance audio quality, Premiere Elements incorporates new effects such as reverb, vocal enhancer, and "dehummer." To add some flair to the video portion of the content, the app has also included new graphics.

Additionally, Adobe has revealed that the Elements Organizer's companion apps for mobile and web include creative overlays, one-click picture repairs, and auto-syncing of images and videos. There is presently only an English-language beta available for these three features.

CHAPTER ONE

The Panel Bin

To hide or show the Panel Bin, select Window > Panel Bin. In the Custom Workspace, go to the section where you want to remove a panel. Then, drag the title bar of that panel into the Panel Bin. You can also rearrange it by dragging the title bar to another location.

To expand or collapse a panel in the panel bin, double-click its name. You can also use other panels outside the bin in the Custom Workspace.

To open a panel, go to the window menu and choose the name of the one that you want to open. Then, click the arrow next to "More" in the taskbar.

To close a panel, go to the window menu and choose the name of the one that you want to close. Then, click the Close button in the title bar.

Drag any corner of the panel to change its size. You can also group one panel with multiple tabs by dragging it onto the target panel's body. A thick line will appear around the target panel's body once the pointer is placed over the correct area for the grouping process. If you want to split a panel into two, drag the one from the outside group to the other one.

Drag the title bar to move a group of panels. Double-click the title bar to expand or collapse a group of panels. You can also dock multiple stacked panels by dragging the tabs of one or more of them to the bottom of another. When the pointer is over the target panel's correct area, a double line appears at its base.

To change the default positions of the panels, go to the Window > Panel menu and choose Reset. You can use the Taskbar to perform this process.

The taskbar features buttons that show the most frequently used operations and panels while working on images in the Photoshop Elements. You can use the tool options and photo bin to switch between the displayed tools and thumbnails. You can also undo or redo operations, rotate the photos, or change the layout of the panels.

The organizer button is located in the upper right corner of the screen. You can also access the home screen using the button located there. In the Expert Mode, you can select the option to switch between the two styles of workspace.

Use the Photo Bin

The Photo Bin is located above the taskbar and is useful for keeping track of all of your open photos. It can be used to switch between multiple photos in your workspace, and it has various controls that allow you to open or close photos, hide them, navigate through them, rotate them, or duplicate them. You can use its Quick mode to quickly bring these photos into your editing process.

Windows only allows you to open an image by dragging it from your computer or other storage device to the Photo Bin.

Drag a thumbnail to move the opened image forward and center it, or change the arrangement of the photos in the photo bin. The order of the photos in the Elements Organizer does not change.

After hiding an image, double-click it in the photo bin and choose "Show in the gallery" from the context menu. Alternatively, right-click and choose "Restore."

Right-click a photo in the photo bin and choose Close. To hide it in a floating window, select Minimize from the menu.

To view a photo's file information, click on a thumbnail and choose the File Info option from the context menus.

Right-click a thumbnail and choose "Duplicate" from the context menu. Then, choose the name of the file you want to copy.

To change the arrangement of the photo, right-click the thumbnail and choose the Rotate option from the context menu.

In the context menu, choose the Show Filenames option to show the file names and other information in the photo bin.

The Show Grid feature shows a grid around photos in the photo bin.

You can create albums containing photos in the photo bin by right-clicking and choosing "Save as Album." The new album appears in the Organizer.

The Show Grid feature displays a grid-like arrangement of photos within the Photo Bin.

Create a new blank file

In this case, you'll need to create a blank file to start with. You can then use this to create a web graphic, company logo, or banner.

To create a new blank file, go to the File > New > Blank File section and choose the options for the new image.

The settings that you can set for the height, width, and resolution of the images that you want to use for print or on screen are included in the list. You can also select the Clipboard option to use the resolution and size of the data that you copied to it.

Size

The list of standard sizes that are available for the selected option displays the options.

Unless you have copied the data to the clipboard, the default values will be based on the last image that you made.

Color Mode

Sets the image to either grayscale, color, or bitmap in 1 bit mode.

The default color of the image's background layer is white. You can change this setting to use the current color or to make it transparent. New images will have a layer 1 instead of a background layer if you set this option.

Right-clicking the image's background can change the type of background color that you want.

Open a file

Import or open images in different file formats. The list of supported formats appears in the Open box, the Import submenu, and the Open As box.

To open a file in Elements Organizer, go to the task bar, select it, and then click the "editor" button.

Navigate to the directory where you want to store the file and select the one that you want to open. You can also check the boxes labeled "All Formats" if the file doesn't open.

To view recent opened files, go to the Open drop-down, which is located above the tool box.

Drag and drop an image from your local directory or device's storage area into the Editor. In the pop-up dialog box, set the specific options for the type of file format that you want to open.

A file can be opened using the Application Frame in macOS.

Sometimes, when using Photoshop Elements, the program may not be able to determine which file format is the right one for your work. For instance, if you're transferring a file from Windows to Mac, the format might be incorrectly labeled.

In the Application Frame, drag a file from anywhere on your computer to the desired location. You can also drag pictures from the Photo Browser or any device that's connected to your computer.

Drag and drop a file into the Application Frame and it will open as a floating document window. You can also convert the open files into floating documents to view them in the Application Frame.

In the Open Recently EDITed File menu, select Preferences and then choose the number of files that you want to save. You can also enter the text box in the Recent File List to view the files that have been opened recently.

In the Preferences section, select the type of file format that you want to open and set the specific options for it.

In the Open Recently Added File submenu, select the number of files that you want to save. Then, enter the text box that appears in the Recent File List containing the number of files that you want to save.

You can specify the file format that you want to use when opening it.

Navigate to the Open As menu and choose the format that you want to use.

If the file doesn't open at all, the chosen format might not match the actual format of the file.

Open a PDF file

PDF is a type of file that can be used to represent various types of data, such as bitmaps and vector files. It is the primary format used by Adobe Acrobat.

The Import PDF dialog box allows you to preview the pages and images from a multi-page PDF file before deciding whether to open them in Photoshop. You can either choose to import all of the pages or just the images from the file. The resolution, color mode, and size of the images can be changed if you import all of them.

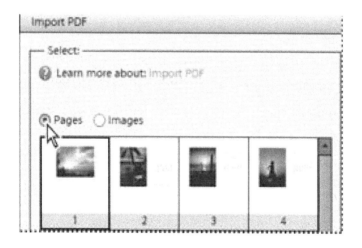

When importing documents from a PDF file, the pages will be displayed in a different format.

The pages are displayed as thumbnails. To change the size of the thumbnails, go to the menu item Thumbnail Size.

To open a PDF file, go to the File > Open menu. You can also change the type of files that are shown in the list.

To import only the images from the file, go to your desired area, select the option, and click the "Import" button. You can also select multiple images from the list, or choose the ones that you want to open individually. If you want to import only the pages, skip this step.

To import multiple pages from a PDF file, go to the "Pages" option in the import dialog box and choose the option that you want to use.

If the file has multiple pages, select the one that you want to open and click OK. To open multiple pages, right-click each one and select "Multiple pages" from the list.

In the Name box, type a new name or accept the existing one. You can also choose to have the image's edges treated with anti-aliasing.

You can set the height and width of the pages to avoid image distortion caused by the changing size. You can also enable constraint ratios to prevent the distortion.

Change the resolution to 300 dpi or choose a new value. Increasing the resolution will increase the file size.

You can set the mode to automatically change the colors in the photos to make them white and black or to keep them in color. If the file has a built-in ICC profile, you can also choose the option from the menu.

To hide any errors that may occur during the import process, select the option to suppress warnings. After that, click OK to open the file.

Placing pages or images from a PDF file into a new layer can be done with the help of this feature. However, you can't change the text or vector data within the artwork because it's bitmapped.

Navigate to the image you want to place and click on the "Place" button.

After selecting the desired page, click OK to open the PDF file. If you want to place multiple pages in a single PDF file, select the one you want to place from the drop-down list.

The artwork that's placed inside a box located at the center of a Photoshop Elements image appears in the box. It retains its original aspect ratio. But, if the size of the artwork exceeds that of the Photoshop image, it's adjusted to fit.

You can reposition the artwork by dragging and placing the pointer inside the box.

Scale the arrangement by dragging one of the handles along the sides or corners of the bounding box.

In the tool options bar, enter the values for H and W to set the height and the width of the artwork. Although these options are usually calculated as percentages, you can also enter different units of measurement such as centimeters, inches, or pixels. To set the proportions of the image, click the "Constrains" box.

You can also rotate the artwork by dragging it along the sides or corners.

To reposition the pointer, position it outside the box where the artwork is placed.

Drag the pointer to the Angle option in the options bar.

Hold down the Command key and drag the box's side handle to get the artwork skewed.

To blend the edges of the image during the process of Rasterization, select the option that's labeled Anti-alias. Then, select the option that's labeled Hard-edged Transition.

After selecting the desired artwork, click the "Commit" button to add it to a new layer.

Process multiple files

The command "Process Multiple Files" can be used to apply specific settings to a folder. If you have a scanner that has a document feeder, you might also be able to process multiple images. You might require an acquire plug in module for this.

When processing files, they can be opened, closed, or saved as modified versions. You can also choose to save the modified versions to a new location or leave the originals unchanged. If you're transferring the processed files to another location, you can create a new folder to hold the saved files.

The command does not work when processing multiple pages of a document. You can start the process by selecting the files that you want to process from the list in the right-hand column. You can then click on the folder that you want to process the images in. You can also import the images from a scanner or digital camera.

You can also choose to include all folders in the process. This will allow you to process files in the specified subdirectories.

Navigate to the destination and select the folder where the processed files will be stored.

Select the destination and specify the type of file-naming conventions that you want to use for the processed files.

In the Rename Files option, select the elements from the pop-up menus or enter text in the fields to merge them into the default names for the files. The fields allow you to change the order of the components of the file's name. You should also include at least one unique field for each of the files to prevent them from overwriting one another.

The starting number for the various fields in the serial number system is specified in the first instance. For instance, if you select the "Serial Letter" option from the menu, the fields will start with the letter "A."

Choose the operating systems that you want to make files compatible with.

Under Image Size, select the Resize option and specify the uniform size that you want for each of the processed files. You can also select the resolution option and set the Constrain Proportions to ensure that the height and width of the photos are proportional.

You can apply an automatic fix to the images by selecting the Quick Fix option from the menu.

You can add a label to the photos by choosing the option from the Labels section. You can customize the text, font size, position, opacity, and other features of the image. You can also change the color of the text by pressing the "change color swatch" button.

You can add a permanent watermark to the photos by selecting the option from the options bar. You can also customize the type of watermark that you want to apply.

To keep track of all the errors that occurred during the process, select the "Log errors" option from the menu. A message will appear after the procedure has been completed if the errors are logged. To review the affected files, open them with a text editor.

After completing the process, click OK to save the files.

Close a file

In the following step, click OK to proceed and save the files after completing the process. In the Photoshop

Elements, select the File > Close option and then choose the option "Save All." You can also decide whether to save the entire file or just the selected part.

Rulers, guides, and grids can help you position various items, such as shapes and layers, in precise positions across the width and length of the image. In contrast, only grids are supported in Quick mode.

Rulers are displayed in the top and left portions of the active window. The markers in the ruler help you determine the position of the pointer when it is moved. You can change the origin of the ruler to determine the grid's point of origin.

The View menu allows you to hide or show the various elements, such as the guide, ruler, or grid. It can also enable or disable the snap of items to the grids or guides.

You can modify the settings and zero origin of rulers.

In Expert mode, you can change the zero origin of rulers. To do so, you can place the pointer over the midpoint of the ruler and drag it diagonally across the image. Then, a set of cross hairs will appear, which will mark the new origin. Release the mouse button to reveal the new zero origin.

Double-click the ruler in the upper-left corner to reset its origin.

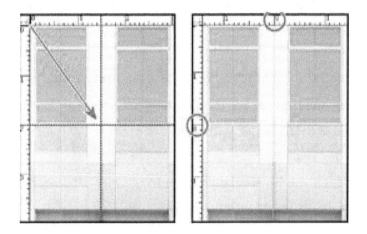

Rulers need to be created from the ground up. This is done by dragging.

Changing the units in the Info panel will automatically update the rulers' units. To change the settings for the guides and grids, go to the Preferences and choose the "Guides & Grids" option. You can also customize the color of the guides or grids by selecting a preset or clicking on the swatch.

To change the settings for the rulers, go to the Preferences and choose the "Units & Rulers" option. For the rulers, choose the unit of measurement.

You can choose the style of the grid lines that you want to use. You can use solid lines or choose from Dashed lines or broken lines.

Enter the value of the number you want to set for gridline every and then choose the measurement unit to define the spacing of the major grid lines.

In subdivisions, enter the value of the number that you want to set for minor grid lines frequency.

Enhanced Quick Mode

The Quick Mode is designed to quickly fix various aspects of an image, such as exposure, color, and sharpness. It features tools such as Quick Actions, Effects, Frames, and Textures, and these can be used to transform your photos.

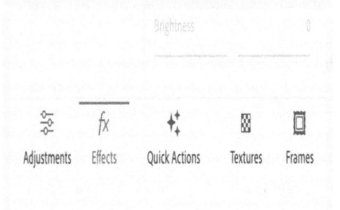

The latest innovations in Adobe Photoshop Elements.

Automated photo editing, AI, and a completely revamped experience make it easy to fix photos. You can easily match the tone or color of any image, or choose a sky or background. For a more unique look, try adding stylized text or experimenting with artistic effect options.

You can easily share photos with friends and family using fast-moving photo reels. With an updated look and a variety of easy-to-use features, you can enjoy a whole new way to share photos. You can also get creative with the new one-click overlays in the web app or the companion app for iOS.

CHAPTER TWO

Dark and light modes have been added

The new UI design of this app brings a modern and easy-to-use experience with a variety of colors and fonts that are designed to make your work easier. You'll also notice a new set of tools and features, such as the Action Bar, toolbar, and buttons.

Color Match

Use built-in settings or photos of your own to customize the brightness, saturation, and color of your pictures. In the Advanced and Quick modes, you can explore the new feature that allows you to color match your photos.

In the Quick mode, select from the built-in presets and adjust the brightness, saturation, or hue.

In the advanced mode, you can add your own custom photo as a preset. This will also help you customize the results.

Photo Reel

Each reel has its own graphics, effects, and text, and it can be saved as GIF or MP4.

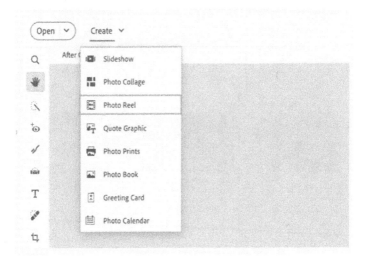

Add Text Guided Edit

This release brings together all the text options into a simple edit that's designed to be easy to follow. You can align text vertically, horizontally, or on a shape or path. You can also style it with patterns and gradients.

This feature allows you to easily customize your photos by going to the guided mode and selecting the Add Text option in the Basics category. Then, follow the guided steps to complete the task.

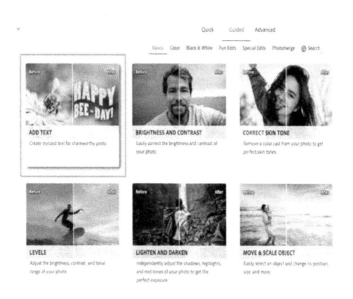

Quick Actions

Quick Actions is a panel that gives you 25 of the most common one-click edits. You can quickly blur, remove background, dehaze, or colorize photos using this feature. It's located next to Effects.

Some of the most popular one-click edits that you can perform in Quick Actions are: removing background, auto smart fix, smoothing skin, and removing JPEG artifacts.

Free Adobe Stock Photos

With thousands of free stock photos in Photoshop Elements, you can create a variety of unique and beautiful quotes, backgrounds, and collages.

These four PSE workflows will help you download free backgrounds and images using the Adobe Stock program. You can also use the Expert mode to customize the background and create a quote graphic.

Enjoy your photos and videos on different devices with the automatic sync feature.

With the new Artistic Effects, you can transform photos into art with a variety of effects that are inspired by popular art styles and famous works.

One-click selection

One-click access to a sky or background allows you to easily modify it. With automatic selections, you can add or remove just one area.

One-click access to the sky or background can be used in two different ways. You can select the subject or the background from the list in the Select menu.

From the Tools panel, you can open any of the selection tools and choose the subject, background, or Sky you want.

CHAPTER THREE

Customize workspace

You can hide certain parts of the workspace or show other areas to accommodate your needs.

To hide or show the Tool Options or the photo bin, go to the bottom of the screen and select the icons that are there.

To split-screen a photo on one side and an edited one on the other, go to Quick mode, and then choose one of the options for View.

In the Organizer and Photo Editor workspace, context menus can be used to display commands that are specific to the program or panel that you're working on. These menus can also be used to access the main ones.

Position the pointer over a panel or image. Note that some panels do not have context menus. To select a command, go to the menu and use the keyboard or the modifier keys.

In the Organizer and Photo Editor workspace, you can use keyboard shortcuts to perform various actions. These shortcuts allow you to quickly and easily execute commands, and they can also be used to modify the way a tool operates.

To learn more about keyboard shortcuts, see the list of shortcuts for tools and modes. You can also save photos and add them to Elements Organizer. Doing so allows you to easily change an image's appearance and save it as an attachment.

Go to the Save dialog box and select the "Add image to elements organizer" option.

To close the two workspace, go to the "Tools" tab and select "Close" from the list. Doing so will automatically close both the Organizer and Photo Editor.

Follow these steps from anywhere in the workspace.

In Windows, go to the File > Exit option and choose "Quit Photoshop Elements." On the Mac, go to the File > Preferences and choose "Quit Photoshop Elements."

To close Photoshop Elements, go to the upper-right portion of the workspace and click the Close button. You can also choose to save all of the files that you've modified. To switch the application's UI color mode to dark or light, go to the Preferences and select "Change UI Color."

In the app, you can learn how to set the Preferences in the Photoshop Elements. You can switch between Dark and

Light modes by going to the Preferences section and selecting either option.

In the Preferences section, click on the "General" button.

To customize the program, select the Light or Moon icon from the menu and click the Preferences button.

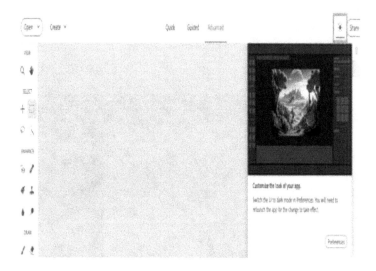

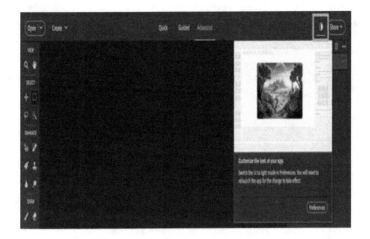

In Photoshop Elements, switch to the light mode.

Upon clicking on the Preferences button, you will be asked to select the UI mode that you want.

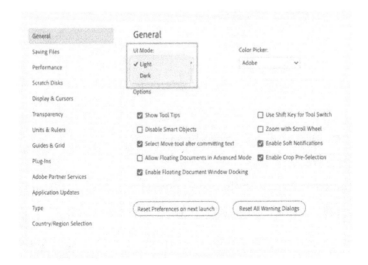

In the Adobe Photoshop Elements program, choose the Dark or Light mode. Then, a message will appear asking you to relaunch the application.

To notify users about the program's relaunch, click on the "Change" button in the dialog box. Then, go back to the application and make the change.

Although the interface of panels in both Elements Organizer and Photoshop Elements is similar, they behave differently. Some of them have menus that allow you to modify or manage images. In Expert mode, you can group them into sections or utilize the Panel Bin to keep them organized.

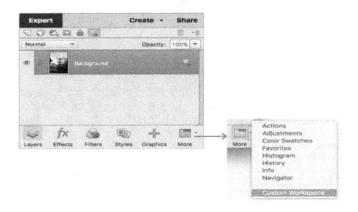

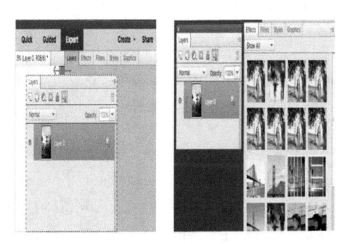

The menu bar and the panel menu have some of the same commands, but some are exclusive to the menus. To view the other commands in the different panels, click the menu button.

You can pop up different sliders in panels with this feature.

In some dialog boxes and panels, there are settings that allow you to pop up different sliders. For instance, in the Layers panel, you can use the Opacity option to customize the appearance of the layer. To activate the pop-up, go to the text box's location and click the triangle. Then, hold down the button and drag the slider to the desired value, or click outside the box.

When the pop-up slider is opened, hold down the Shift key and click the Down or Up arrow to set or decrease values.

There are several ways to enter values. To open a window, click the "Open" button. Then, go to the text box and click the "Change" button. You can also click the "Add" button to add a new value.

Work with panels, which come in logical groups and contain information, features, or functions, quickly and easily. The right-hand panel bin is located in the Photoshop Elements application's section. It displays tabs and panels according to the mode that you're in.

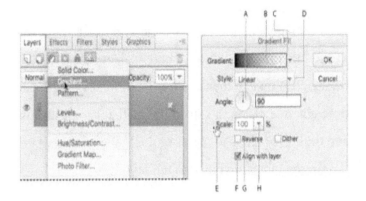

The Quick mode provides a list of the quick-mode techniques that can be used to apply a photo's effects. On the other hand, the Guided mode allows you to select the various edits that you want to make in a specific panel. In the Expert context, the options for a particular panel are listed. There are two ways to view these panels: Basic Workspace and Custom Workspace.

The default workspace is the Basic Workspace. It features various buttons for panels that are frequently used. These include Favorites, Effects, Graphics, and Layers. To see all of the available tabs or close them, click the More button.

Custom Workspace

To view the panels in a tab-based layout, click the arrow next to the More button and select the Custom Workspace. You can then view a list of the available tabs and select one from the drop-down list. You can also group multiple panels together or dock one of them. Drag and drop the tabs' title bar into the layout.

If you want to remove a panel from the Panel Bin, you can do so by dragging it out.

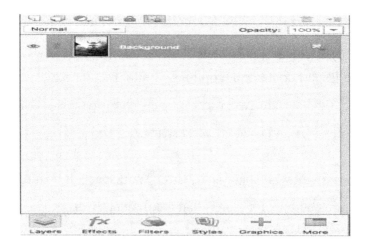

Chapter FOUR

Home screen

The first thing you will see after launching Adobe Photoshop Elements is the Home screen. This is where you can open the program and view various features, get in touch with the latest version of the software, and view tutorials. You can also learn more about the Home screen by going to the "Get to know the Elements" page.

The Welcome screen for 2018 and earlier versions of Photoshop Elements will automatically appear if you are using the program.

The Welcome screen will open automatically once you start Photoshop Elements. It's a convenient place to start and tackle various tasks.

To open the welcome screen, click on it. Enhance your photos with the Photo Editor, or add special effects with this tool.

To open the photo editor in its default mode, go to the icon and click it.

To open the photo editor, go to the drop-down menu and choose the type of file that you want to open.

Import, organize, or set up your photos using the Organizer feature. With the Video Editor, you can create and enhance videos with fun effects.

To close the welcome screen, go to the upper-right portion of the screen and click the Close button. It's not necessary to go back to the Welcome screen if you want to open other workspaces.

The Settings icon will be shown next to the Close button. It will determine which application to open when you start.

Photoshop Elements window

The eLive view is a tool that allows users to access content and resources from within the editor and organizer of Photoshop Elements. It features a variety of channels that are categorized into three main categories: Learn, Inspire, and News. To search for specific articles or videos, simply click the search icon and enter your query.

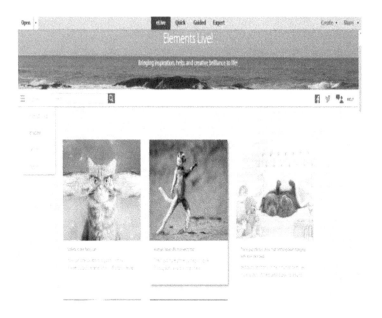

The articles will be shown automatically. You can filter the content for channels that you want to focus on, such as learning, inspiration, and news quick.

In the Quick mode, you can easily make quick and simple adjustments to your photos. These include changing the exposure, sharpness, and color of photos.

The Enhanced Quick mode is additionally available.

The guided mode allows you to control photos using a wizard-like interface. It features predefined effects that can be applied to them. The associated images show the effect when the user hovers over it.

Expert

With this feature, you can enhance photos in the Expert mode.

In the Expert mode, you can create special effects, fix color issues, and enhance photos. There are also simple tools for lighting and color correction in Quick mode. In the guided mode, you can learn more about photography and basic photo editing.

If you're new to digital imaging, the guided or Quick modes can help you fix photos.

If you're a seasoned user of image-editing applications, you'll find the Expert mode to be versatile and powerful. It includes command-line tools for color correction and lighting, as well as a variety of other functions, such as painting and adding text and fixing image defects.

The Expert workspace can be rearranged to accommodate your needs. You can hide, move, and show panels within the Panel Bin. In addition, you can zoom in or out of a photo, change the view of the document, and create multiple windows.

The main tabs are the active, inactive, and options bars. The toolbox, options bar, photo bin, and taskbar are also included. The panel bar is the final section.

The menus are organized according to the topics they serve. For instance, the Enhance menu offers commands that enable the application of adjustments to images.

The mode selector provides buttons that allow users to select the three different editing options. It also contains the Open and Create drop-down menus.

The toolbox holds tools that are used to enhance images. The panel bin organizes the various features and actions into logical groups.

The menu features the option to display and manage the photos in the photo bin and the tools options to set the parameters of the chosen tool.

The taskbar is a convenient area where users can quickly access the actions they've used most frequently.

CHAPTER FIVE

Effects

The Effects panel is a single location where you can apply various types of effects to a photo. It's located on the taskbar and features a variety of categories and subcategories. The first category is labeled "Artistic," while the second is "Classic," and the third is "Color Match."

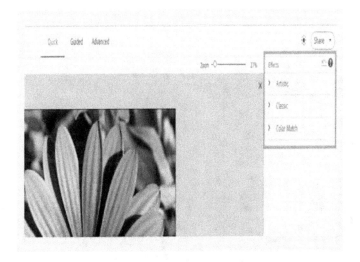

Artistic Effects

Transform your photos into works of art with creative effects inspired by popular styles and works of art using just a single click. You can choose from a variety of effects that are designed to fit any part of your image and easily adjust its results. These effects can be accessed in Advanced and Quick modes.

In addition, five new artistic effects were added to Photoshop Elements 2024.

Classic effects

There are 55 classic effects in this collection, ranging from vintage to black and white. You can view the available variations by selecting a classic effect.

Through its analysis of the available image, this tool can provide various effects based on the content.

The Auto models are Auto1, Auto2, Auto3, Auto4, and Auto5.

The effects are applied using a mask on a new layer. In Advanced mode, you can modify the mask's settings to remove or minimize the effects from specific areas.

The effect provides a color tint to the image, such as green, sepia, and golden. The variations are as follows: • Sepia • Golden • Copper • Green • Blues Seasons • Spring • Autumn • Winter • Snow Pencil Sketch • which makes the image look like a pencil sketch.

Differentiations include: Soft Lines, Pencil Sketch, Stippling, and Colored Pencil Toy Camera.

This effect makes the image look similar to a toy camera's snapshot.

The effect provides a color tint to the image, such as green, golden, and sepia. The variations are as follows: • Sepia • Golden • Copper • Green • Blues Seasons • Spring • Autumn • Winter • Snow Pencil Sketch.

Variations include: Soft Lines, Pencil Sketch, Charcoal, and the Colored Pencil Toy Camera.

The effect can make an image look like a photo taken by a toy camera, with different variations available.

Differentiations are as follows: Lomo Blue, Lomo Contrast, and Holga Black & White. The effect of black and white on an image can be applied with variations offered by Simple B & W, Old School, Platinum, and Tinted Black Lithograph.

The effect involves processing a photographic film using a chemical solution that's designed for a different kind of film.

The various types of washes include deep blue, orange, purple, and green.

Split Tone

The effect involves adding a contrasting color to an image's highlights and shadows.

Differentiations for this effect include: Split Tone, Red Tone, Green Tone, and Vintage. Effects that are related to vintage are available in variations. Some of these include fading, vintage leak, and Sepia Glow.

This effect applies light to the negative of an image that has been leaked inside a camera's light-tight chamber.

The leaked image's negative can be divided into three categories: tarnished colors, soft leaks, and yellow streaks.

Color Match effects

You can use a photo of your own or select from built-in presets to enhance saturation, brightness, and color balance. You can explore the effects in Quick and Advanced modes.

In quick mode, apply the color match effect.

Select the built-in presets that are available in the Color Match section of the Effects panel.

In the File > Open option, choose the photo that you want to apply the effect to.

The Color Match effects are exclusive and will not be used on the main input photo. This means that any presets that were applied to the photo will be replaced with those from another preset.

If you want to apply a particular preset over another, then you can do so in either of the two ways.

After saving the results of your first preset, use it as an input photo for the next one.

In Quick mode, choose the first preset and then switch to Advanced. In the Advanced mode, use the results from Quick mode to input your photo. Then, choose the appropriate one from the list.

You can also customize the brightness, saturation, and Hue of your photos depending on your requirements.

To cancel or redo the edits, go to the Undo button and select the Redo option. You can also save the image as a file or choose to share it on social media.

You can also customize the appearance of your photo using the texture panel. There are ten different types of textures that you can choose from which simulate various backgrounds or surfaces.

Enhance the texture of your photos with this preset.

A layer mask is used to add texture to a photo. In Advanced mode, you can modify the mask's appearance to remove or minimize it from certain areas of the face or skin.

Frames

The frames panel allows you to choose and apply from the various types of frames that are available for your photo. You can also double-click the frame to change its appearance or move it. In Advanced mode, you can modify the background color to any other choice.

You can apply various effects and textures on a photo using the Photoshop Elements editor. Open the picture and choose Quick mode from the menu.

Besides the Adjustments panel, there are also three additional panels that are available: Effects, Frames, and Textures. To select the icons for these panels, go to the settings and then click on the appropriate option.

The preview pane of the Panel bar shows live previews of the photos that you've selected. You can click on the desired effect or texture to apply it.

After choosing Quick mode, go to Advanced and customize the way you used the image's texture, effect, or frame. You can also add a separate layer to the modification that you want to make.

The metadata of the file is related to its information.

When you take a snapshot of your digital camera, the information in the image file, which is referred to as metadata, includes various details about the photo, such as its date and time, aperture, shutter speed, and the model of the camera. You can view and add this data in the Properties section of the Elements Organizer or the File Info dialog box in Photoshop Elements.

In addition to the usual metadata, you can add other information such as a title, description, and keyword tags to help identify your photos as you organize and manage them. As you perform various tasks, such as editing a file, Photoshop Elements will track the history of the changes that have been made.

When a Digimarc watermark is detected, the image files are automatically scanned. If the copyright symbol is present, the title bar of the image will show a copyright symbol. There will also be information related to the copyright status, notices, and URL sections of the File info dialog box.

You can add a visual watermark to your photos to indicate that they're your own work. However, these aren't stored in the information of the file.

You can view or add the information in the image file in the Properties section of the Elements Organizer or in the File Info dialog box in the Photoshop Elements editor.

The dialog box displays information about the camera data, including the model, model number, and caption. You can modify or add this data to the file in Photoshop Elements using this dialog box. The embedded metadata that you add is stored using XMP, which is a standard metadata platform.

The Extensible Markup Language (XMP) is a standard that enables third-party applications and workflows to create, process, and exchange documents' metadata. If you have multiple metadata entries for different files, then you can create templates that help you add information to them more quickly.

The Camera Data category doesn't allow you to modify the information displayed within it.

When you add a keyword to a file in the photo browser's File Info dialog box, it appears as a keyword. However, some file formats, such as those used in the PDF and BMP files, do not support this feature.

To change the information displayed in the image file, go to the File > File Info section and click on the "Browse" button. You can also right-click on a thumbnail in the photo bin and choose the category.

On the top-right corner of the dialog box, click on the Description tab and choose the topic that you want to view. You can add or modify the text boxes and the information that's displayed in the Description section. You can also choose the drop-down list that's related to the copyright status.

Efficiency

Use the Info panel

The Expert mode displays information about an image, such as its file name and color value, beneath the pointer. In addition, this panel displays other details depending on the program being used.

To view the information in the Info panel while dragging an image, make sure that it is visible in your workspace.

To view the Info panel, go to the Window > Info option.

Go to the tool selection and choose the one that you want to use. Drag or move the pointer to the image or within it to use it. Depending on which tool you're using, the following information might appear.

The value of the pointer's color under it and its coordinates are shown in the form of numbers.

Drag the width or height of a shape or a big or rectangular item as you do so. The active selection's active width and height will also be shown.

The starting position of the object you're working on will be shown in the form of coordinates.

The coordinate changes caused by the movement of a layer, shape, or selection will be shown in the y and x axes.

The axes represent the axes of rotation and the angle of line or gradient. The axes also show the changes caused by the movement of a layer or a selection.

The axes represent the angle of a gradient or line, the rotation axis, or the change in its angle as an object moves.

The percentage change in the height and width of a selection, layer, or shape as you scale it will be shown in the form of H and W. The angle of vertical or horizontal skew will be shown as you skew it.

To change the mode of the values displayed, go to the pop-up menu and choose the appropriate option. You can also set the parameters of the color reading process in the panel's More section.

Grayscale

The grayscale values under the pointer can be shown using the symbol Grayscale. The value of the RGB color, which is represented by the letters R, Y, and Z, can also be displayed using the symbol Web Color. The HSB value, which is represented by the letters H, S, and X, can also be shown using the symbol.

You can change the type of measurement that's displayed in the unit of measurement by choosing it from the menu's pop-up option or by going to the More section and choosing the Panel Options option.

The status bar or the Info panel can display information about a particular file.

In the status bar or the Info panel, you can modify the information that's displayed. The leftmost section shows the current magnification, while the section next to it displays the current file information.

Go to the More menu and select the Panel Options option from the drop-down list.

Navigate to the Info panel's More menu and select the Panel Options option. Then, choose the view option for documents.

Document Sizes

The information displayed shows the overall size of the image's data. The leftmost number represents the printing size, while the rightmost number shows the file's actual size, as well as its layers.

The name of the image's color profile is displayed as the Document Profile. The Document Dimensions is a representation of the data's size in the selected units.

Scratch Sizes

The amount of RAM and scratch disk space that Photoshop Elements uses to process the image is displayed. Left indicates how much memory is currently being used, while right shows the available memory for processing images.

Efficiency

The percentage of time it takes to perform an operation compared to the amount of time spent on writing and reading from scratch disks is displayed. If the value is less than 100%, the program is using the disk less efficiently.

The time it took to complete a particular operation is displayed. The current tool's name is shown, and the save or delete option is also displayed.

You can save the entries in the metadata templates for the items that you repeatedly enter in the File Info dialog box. These templates can help minimize the amount of time that you spend on retyping the information in the box. The Photo Browser also lets you search for related metadata.

Navigate to the File Info dialog box and open the program. You can then view the current operation's details and the save or delete option.

To save the metadata in a template, go to the drop-down list and select the Export option. Then, enter the name of the template you want to save.

To remove a specific metadata template, go to the Show templates folder and click the "Remove" button.

You can use a saved template for preserving metadata.

Go to the File Info dialog box and click the drop-down button. You can then choose the import option to add the specified metadata to your file.

After selecting the import option, click OK.

After selecting the import option, click OK. You can then choose a template from the saved templates list.

The pop-up panels that appear in the tool options bar are designed to provide access to a variety of predefined libraries. These are called presets and can be used to customize the look of your projects. When the panels are closed, they show a thumbnail of the selected preset.

You can change the appearance of the pop-up panel's preview to show pre-defined icons or preset names.

The Presets Manager can be used to load various predefined libraries. They are stored in separate files and can be accessed by navigating to the "Presets" folder in the application folder of Photoshop Elements.

In the options bar, choose the type of tool that you want to use. Then, click the pop-up panel's menu icon. You can then view and select the currently loaded libraries or click on an item in the list to pick a preset.

In the pop-up menu, choose the "Save Brush" option and enter the name of your desired brush.

In the panel menu, choose the "New Gradient" or "New Pattern" option. Then, enter the name of the template that you want to save.

You can change the name of a gradient, pattern, or brush in a panel by going to the pop-up menu and choosing the "Rename command" option.

To remove a gradient, a brush, or a pattern from a panel, go to the pop-up menu and select the "Delete command" from the list. You can also hold down the Alt key and click the desired object.

The pop-up panel's menu can be used to save a collection of patterns, gradients, or brushes. In the menu, choose the "Save Brushes," "Save Gradients," or "Save Pattern" command, and then enter the name of the library file that you want to save.

Load a collection of patterns, gradients, or brushes by going to the pop-up menu and choosing the "Load command" option. You can then select the files that you want to add.

The Load option can add a new library to your current collection of brushes. If you're planning on using a preset, the new library will replace the ones currently in use.

In the Append section, click the "Add" button and choose the files that you want to append.

To change the current selection of gradient patterns in a panel, click the menu's pop-up icon and choose the library that you want to load. You can also click the Load command to add the new library or browse to its location.

To replace the existing collection of patterns or brushes in a panel, go to the Brushes menu and choose a library.

The current collection of patterns, gradients, and brushes may be replaced with the selection of the Preset Manager from the menu. Alternatively, you can load a different set of files by choosing the option to use the tool.

Load the default collection of brushes or gradients by going to the pop-up menu and choosing the Reset option.

You can change the way items are displayed in the pop-up menu.

Go to the Preset Manager and click the More button to change the display of all panels.

You can customize the way items are displayed by choosing the View option. Text only displays the name of each item, while large and small thumbnails show the name and details of each item. On the other hand, the Stroke Thumbnail option displays a sample stroke and the brush size.

The Preset Manager is a tool that allows you to manage the libraries of various types of pre-defined tools, such as color swatches, effects, gradients, and patterns in

Photoshop Elements. You can create a group of favorite brushes or restore the default ones.

The different types of libraries in Photoshop Elements come with their own file extensions and default folders. The files are installed automatically on your computer when installed.

The Preset Manager allows users to remove a preset by selecting it and clicking on the Delete button. The Reset option can also be used to restore the selected items to the original state.

Load a library

Select styles, effects, gradients, patterns, or brushes from the menu in the Preset Manager.

From the list, click on the Add button, and then select the library you want to load. If you want to load it from another folder, go to that folder, and then select the library. The default is that the pre-set files are placed in the Presets folder of Photoshop Elements.

From the menu, click on the More button, and then choose the library that you want to load. You can then click the Done button to restore or remove it. In the Preset Manager's menu, click the More button, and choose the command "Reset the default library."

In the Preset Manager, select multiple non-contiguous presets using the Ctrl-click or Shift-click option. The selected ones will be saved in the new library.

After you have selected the library, enter its name and click Save. If you want to use the library in a different folder, navigate to that folder first.

Rename a preset

In the list of the Preset Manager, select a preset and click Rename. Then double-click it.

New names must be entered for the presets if you have multiple selections.

Multitouch support

If your computer supports Touch, you can use it to zoom in or scroll through an image. You may also tap to enhance, sort, or find photos in the Quick Edit or Organizer modes. There are three different Multitouch modes that are supported: Quick, Expert, and guided.

Flicking

To scroll the image vertically or horizontally, use one of your fingers to touch the screen. You can also move the finger up or down by doing so.

Pinching in or out

To zoom in or out of an image, place one of your fingers on the trackpad on a Mac and pinch. Then, pinch and zoom in to get the two fingers in the right direction.

About scratch disks

When your computer doesn't have enough RAM to run the program, you can use a scratch disk instead. A scratch disk is a partition of a hard drive or any other device that has free memory. The primary one used by Photoshop Elements is the one that's installed on the system.

There are various ways to set up the primary scratch disk. You can change its name or choose to have more than one scratch disk. When the primary is full, use the extra disks. Ensure that the hard disk has plenty of free defragmented space.

Rather than using a remote network drive, you can create scratch disks locally.

You should not create a scratch disk on the same hard drive as the one that holds the virtual memory of the computer.

You should avoid creating scratch disks on the same drive as large files that you are editing or Photoshop Elements.

Follow these guidelines when creating and assigning scratch disks. They will help ensure that the device performs well.

When creating a scratch disk using Photoshop Elements, you need to ensure that there's enough space on the hard drive to accommodate it. Doing so by regularly defragmenting the hard drive can help ensure that there's space available for the scratch disk. You can use a utility such as Windows Disc Defragmenter to do this.

Using a local drive or media that's not removable is the best way to create scratch disks. You can also use RAID disks or arrays for dedicated volumes.

Regularly defragmenting and using an empty drive or a device with plenty of free space can help prevent fragmentation issues.

Change scratch disks

In the list of scratch disks, choose the ones that you want to use.

To change the order in which your scratch disks will be placed, select a particular one and use the arrow key next to it.

After you've selected the desired order, click OK and then restart Photoshop Elements.

About plug in modules

Software developers such as Adobe develop plug-ins that can be used in Photoshop Elements to add various features. There are a variety of import, export, and special effects plug-ins included with the program.

Upon installing the plug-ins, they appear in the Import or Export section of the menu. There are also various filters and file formats in the Save As and Open boxes.

If you have a large number of plug-ins installed, it's possible that Photoshop Elements won't be able to display all of them in the appropriate menus. To prevent this, you should add a tilde character to the start of the plug ins' names, folders, or files. When the program starts, it will automatically ignore files that have this character. To see information about the installed plug-ins, go to the Help section and select a plug in.

To use a plug-in that's not included with the program, go to the folder where the modules are located and copy the one that you want to use from there. Then, install the plug-in and Photoshop Elements.

To install compatible plug-ins that are stored in different applications, select the "additional plug-ins" folder. There, you can create a shortcut for the plug in and use it with Photoshop Elements.

Follow the steps below to install the plug-ins in modules 1. If the installer is provided, follow the instructions to install the software.

Ensure that the files are uncompressed. Then, copy them to the correct location in the Photoshop Elements directory.

Select an additional plug in folder

To load plug-ins that have been created and stored in other applications, go to the additional plug-ins folder.

In both Windows and Mac, go to the Preferences section of the application and select the "plug-ins" category.

Make sure that you don't select the location in the plug-ins directory for Photoshop Elements. After you've installed the plug-in, go back to the main application and restart it.

When the program starts, all of the pre-loaded plug-ins are automatically loaded. The third-party plug-ins that are located in the other plugins-folders will not be loaded. To avoid this, select the "Skip loading optional plug-ins" option from the list of options.

Application Updates

The Windows Application Store doesn't support the option to update the program's version.

The program's Preferences dialog features various update options.

The time when an update is installed in the application is up to you. In some versions of the software, such as Photoshop Elements, you can also set the program's actions when it comes to receiving updates.

To access the program's update dialog, go to the Preferences section and click on the "Application Updates" tab. You can then choose the type of update that you want to receive.

The process of automatically downloading and installing updates works seamlessly. It installs the latest version when the application is restarted.

Notifications are provided when updates are available. The user can opt to delay or start the process of getting the latest version.

The program can perform various actions such as canceling, redo, or undo.

Many of the operations in the Elements Organizer and the Photoshop Elements can be changed or undone. For instance, you can restore the entire image or part of it to its previous version. Unfortunately, with low memory, you can't use these options.

To undo or change an operation, go to the Edit > Undo or choose the Edit Redo option. To cancel an operation from the list of options, hold the Esc key until it stops working. Tapping the History panel while continuing with the operation will show you the past actions.

The History panel allows you to track the recent state of an image. It can be used to look back at the changes that have been made to the image.

In the panel, each of the states of an image will be listed separately. You can select which of these states you want to work in, and the image will revert to how it looked before the changes were made.

The program does not affect the pixels in the image by performing actions such as scrolling and zooming. It also doesn't change the color settings or the panels' properties.

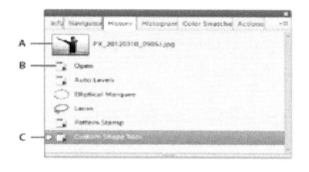

The initial state, followed by a B. State in the history panel, followed by a C. State in the selected category.

The History panel of Photoshop Elements automatically displays the 50 previous states. These older states are deleted from the memory of the application to free up more space. You can set the maximum number of states to 1000 in the settings.

The history panel's top section displays the original state of the image. You can revert it by clicking on its top state. This is handy when comparing the previous and current versions of your work.

After closing and reopening the document, all the states from the previous working session are removed from the panel.

A new state is added to the list at the bottom. The oldest one is at the top, while the newest one is at the bottom.

The state by state list shows the name of the command or tool that can be used to alter the image.

When you select a state, it dims the subsequent states, which indicate the changes that were made after the selected step. This helps you identify which changes were made in the process.

When you select a state, it automatically eliminates the states that were created following it. On the other hand, deleting a state completely eliminates the associated edits.

In Expert and Quick modes, you can revert to the previous state of an image. To do this, go to the History panel and click on the name of the state. You can also click the Redo or Undo buttons in the taskbar.

To set the keyboard command to "Step Forward" and "Step Backward," go to Preferences in Windows and select "General" from the drop-down list, and then choose "From the Step Back/Fwd" from the list.

The undo history panel can be used to remove multiple states.

To remove a state, go to the History panel and click on the name of the one that you want to remove. You can also click the Delete History option to remove the states that were followed by the selected one.

To remove the states from the history panel without changing the image, go to the panel's menu and click on the "Clear History" option. Doing so will help free up some space in the application's memory.

The only reason why you can't unundo the history panel is because it contains traces of your actions. In the Expert mode, you can clear the memory of both the history and the clipboard by removing the items that were copied to them. In the process, you can also free up more space. In the Clipboard Contents section, click the Edit button.

To remove the stored states using the undo history panel, go to the History panel and click on the option to "Clear History."

To completely remove the stored data in both the history and the clipboard, go to the Edit > Clear > All option.

In Quick or Expert modes, you can view and remove the states of images.

You can use the Zoom, Hand, and Navigator tools to magnify an image's different sections.

Various methods can be used to magnify or reduce the view. The title bar of the window displays the zoom percentage, except when the window is too small to fit the display.

If you want to see a different part of an image, you can use the Hand tool or the window's scroll bars. You can also drag and pan the image using the Navigator panel.

When using the Hand tool, hold down the spacebar while dragging within the image.

Drag the Hand tool over the image to reveal another part of it.

Zoom in or out

From the toolbar, select the Zoom tool and click either the Zoom Out or Zoom In button. You can then magnify or reduce the image depending on the setting you want. The resulting display will be centered around the point you selected. If the image's magnification level exceeds 3200%, the magnified glass will not appear.

You can easily magnify an image by dragging a Zoom tool over its part. To do so, select the "Zoom In" button in the options bar. Then, start dragging the image's marquee and hold the spacebar down.

Drag the Zoom slider over the part you want to magnify. In the options bar, click the "View > Zoom Out" or "View > Zoom In." Then, enter the magnification level that you want. You can also switch between zoom in and out by holding down Alt. To display an image at 100%, double-click the Zoom tool.

Go to the tools bar and click the "1" button to choose one of the options. You can also choose the view option or right-click the image to get the actual pixel count. Then, enter the total for the count and press "Enter." You can then fit the image to the screen by double-click the Hand tool.

To choose which option you prefer, click the "1" button in the toolbar. You can also right-click or view the image and choose the actual pixel count option. You can then press "Enter" to complete the task and add the image to your screen. You can double-click one of the tools in the toolbox.

In the options bar, select the Zoom or the Hand tool and click the "Fit Screen" button. Alternatively, right-click the picture and choose "Fit On Screen."

The options that you've selected will determine the size and zoom level of the window that fits the available screen space. You can also resize it while zooming.

When the Zoom tool is active, select the "Resize Windows to Fit" option in the options bar. It will resize the window as you magnify or minimize the effect of the image.

Regardless of the magnification level of the image, the window will remain the same size. This is useful when you use smaller monitors or work with tiled images.

Using the Navigator panel

The Navigator panel allows you to change the area of view and magnification of an image. You can input a value in the text box or click the Zoom In or Zoom Out button to change the magnification level. You can also drag the view box in the thumbnail image to move the view of the picture.

The view box can be changed by choosing the Panel Options from the menu in the Navigator panel. You can pick a color from the menu or click the swatch to open the Color picker. After you've selected a color, click OK.

In the Expert mode, you may open several windows to show different views of a particular file. The list of open windows will appear in the window menu, and the thumbnails of each window will show in the photo bin. Unfortunately, you may only have a limited amount of memory.

Navigate to the New Window option and choose the image file you want to view. If you want to view both the first and second window at the same time, you may have to move the first window to the position where the first one is.

The New Window command can be used to change the appearance of an image in a separate window when working with a zoom-in image.

Arrange your windows to show different views of a particular file.

In the Expert mode, you can display windows in a stack or cascading style from the upper left to the bottom right of the screen.

To show windows evenly across the edges, go to the "Window" > "Images" category and choose "Tiles". When you close the window, it will be resized to fit the available space.

To view every open image at the same magnification, go to the "Window" > "Images" and choose "Match Zoom".

To view the same portion of an image in all of your windows, go to the "Window > Images" category and choose "Match Location." The view in all of your windows will match the most recent active image.

In the Taskbar, click on the Layout option and choose a new layout.

Only the options for Window > Images are enabled in Expert Mode when the preference for allowing floating documents is selected.

In Expert mode, you can close the windows one by one. You can do this by going to the File > Close option and choosing the option that's located in the title bar. You can also click on a photo in the Bin and choose "Close All." The resolution and size of the image are the most important factors that you consider when choosing to close the windows.

The pixel dimensions or image size of an image are the number of pixels that can be found along its height and width. For instance, a digital camera can take a picture with a resolution of 1500x1024 pixels, and it will determine the size of the file.

The resolution is the overall amount of information that's in a given space. It's measured in pixels per inch, and the higher the resolution, the better the print quality. Higher resolution images are usually more detailed.

Even though digital images contain a certain amount of information, they do not have a specific resolution or size. Its physical dimensions and width or height change as you change the resolution.

A pair of images with the same file size and resolution but different picture sizes and resolutions. The higher the resolution, the better the print quality.

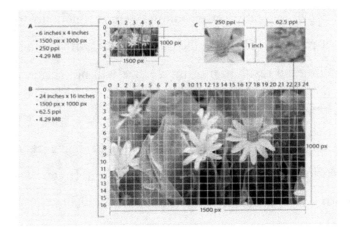

The relationship between the resolution and the image size can be seen in the dialog box's Image Size section. As you change one of the values, the other two will also change.

With the Constrain Proportions feature, you can change the size of an image without affecting its data.

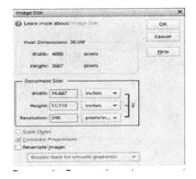

The constraint ratio option allows you to maintain the aspect ratio, which is the height to width of the image. Changing the resolution or image size will not shrink or stretch the picture.

You can change the image's size without changing its resolution using the Resample Image option. If you want to print at a particular resolution or if you want to use a smaller or larger version, you can resample the image, though this method can degrade the quality.

About monitor resolution

The resolution of your monitor is based on its pixel dimensions. For instance, if you set your monitor's resolution to 1600 x 1200, your photo's pixel dimensions will be the same as that of your image. When the image appears on the screen, it will be a size that's proportional to the size of the pixels in the image. In Photoshop Elements you can easily change the magnification of the image.

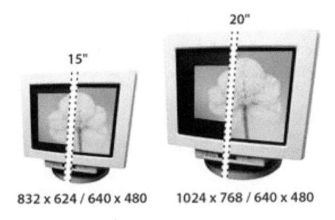

832 x 624 / 640 x 480   1024 x 768 / 640 x 480

An image of 620 x 400 pixels is displayed on different monitors with different resolution and sizes.

When preparing images for use on a TV screen, make sure that the resolution of your monitor is the lowest it will be able to display.

Open files should also be displayed with the appropriate size.

To view the file information box, click on it at the bottom. It displays the various information about the image, such as its height and width, the resolution, and the number of channels.

On the next screen, choose the print size that you want to use. You can also click on the "Tool Options" bar and select the "Print Size" option.

In the Document Size section, select the appropriate magnification for the image and set it to show its actual print size. Be aware that the print size of your monitor may be affected by its resolution and size.

Without resampling, you can change the resolution and print dimensions.

If you're planning on sending the image to a shop that requires a specific resolution, you might need to change the resolution and print dimensions of the file.

This process is not necessary if you're using Photoshop Elements. You can simply choose the size that you want and the application will set the appropriate resolution.

In order to change the resolution, print dimensions, and total pixels in the image, you must first resample it.

Navigate to the "Resize" option and choose the size of the image that you want.

Make sure that you have opted out of resampling. You can still change the resolution and print dimensions without changing the whole image's total number of pixels, but it might not maintain its current proportions.

Select the Resample image to take advantage of the Scale Style and Constrain Proportions functions.

To maintain the aspect ratio's current state, select the "Constrain Proportions" option. This will automatically update the width and height of the image as you change its height.

To change the height and width of the file, go to the Document Size section and enter the new values. You can also choose a new measurement unit if you want.

Go to the "Resolution" option and choose the new measurement type. Then click OK.

To return the values that were displayed in the image size dialog box, use the Alt key and click "reset."

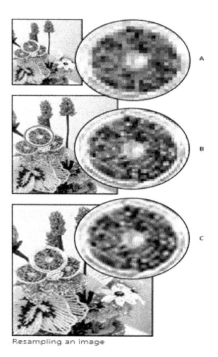

Resampling an image

CHAPTER SIX

Resample an image

Resampling is a process that involves altering an image's pixel dimensions. This can affect its overall image quality and print output, as well as its size on the screen. When you downsample an image, the data in it is lost, and information is removed.

Upsampling or increasing the number of pixels in an image can add new ones based on the values of the old ones, resulting in a loss of detail and sharpness.

To avoid resampling, you can create the image at the appropriate resolution or scan it to get the best possible output. If you want to see how the changes in the resolution will affect the print dimensions, you can try resampleing a duplicate of the file.

You can either downsample an image or upsample it. Downsampling involves extracting the original image while upsampling adds new details.

It is important to specify the size of the image in terms of its pixel dimensions if you are preparing it for web use.

Navigate to the "Resize" option and choose the size of the image that you want. Then, choose the method that you want to use.

This method is generally recommended for creating small files with non-aliased edges. However, it can also create jagged edges that can appear when performing various manipulations.

Bilinear

A bilinear method is ideal for creating smooth tonal gradations. When you're working on increasing the size of an image, a bicubic smoother is preferred.

Bicubic Sharper

This variation maintains the details intact in a resampled version. It may, however exaggerate some areas of the image. You can try using bicubic if this method oversharpens certain parts of the picture.

In the "Pixel Dimensions" section, enter the values of the height and width of the image. You can also select the percentage of the current measurements as the unit of measurement.

After you have selected the desired pixel dimensions, click OK to resample the image.

Crop an image

The new size of the image is next to the Pixel Dimensions section, and the old one is in the parentheses.

To change the crop ratio of the image, select the one that you prefer from the list located at the left-hand side of the tool options panel. You can also set custom values in the Height and Width fields.

The ability to change the image's crop ratio or set custom values in the height and width fields allows you to alter the size of the image.

When the image is cropped, the aspect ratio of the photo is displayed, as well as the values for the cropped image's height and width. The resolution field can be used to change the image's resolution.

The drop-down list displays the Custom option when you specify the values for the height and width of the crop tool.

Drag over the parts of the image you wish to keep. Release the mouse button and the crop marquee will appear as a bounding box enclosing handles at the sides and corners.

You can also customize the appearance of the crop marquee by dragging and dropping parts of the image.

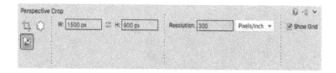

You can change the aspect ratio of the image by selecting the value from the drop-down list located on the left.

To change the position of the crop marquee, click-drag or use the arrow keys to move it.

Drag a handle to resize the marquee. From the drop-down list, choose No Restrictions. You can set the proportions and hold down Shift to get the desired effect.

To swap the values for the height and width of the image, click the "Swap" icon in the options bar. You can also rotate the crop marquee by dragging and dropping it. However, this method can't be used with Bitmap mode.

You can also change the opacity and color of the crop shield by choosing the Preferences option and entering the new value. In the Crop Tool section, click the "Display & Cursors" button and choose "New Color and Opacity". If you want to crop the shield without changing its appearance, select the Use Shield option.

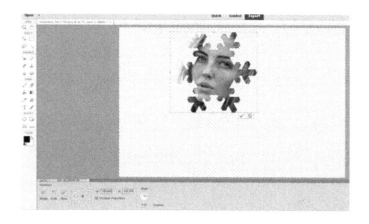

In the lower-right corner, click the green button. You can then double-click the box to finish the cropping process or click the red button to cancel it.

Canvas can be enlarged or shrunk.

The canvas is an area around an image that can be used as a workspace. It can be used to increase or decrease its size. In the context of the image window, the added canvas can be shown in the background layer's default or selected extension color. In other layers, it can be transparent.

You can change the canvas' size.

To determine the size of the canvas, go to the Relative tab, select the number you want, and enter a negative value for the reduction. You can then increase the canvas' size by adding 2 inches to each side.

Go to the Relative tab and select the number you want to add or decrease to the canvas. Then, enter a negative value to decrease its size. You can then use this method to increase the canvas' size, which can be as much as 2 inches.

To see the position you want the canvas to be in, click the arrow next to the anchor icon.

To change the canvas' color, go to the Extensions menu and choose the option that you want.

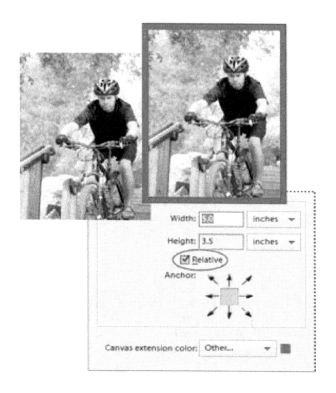

Straighten an image

An improperly aligned image can be caused by camera shake. For instance, if the horizon in a picture of a sunset is not completely horizontal, it can be corrected by using the Straighten tool. In addition to this, you can also crop or resize the image to straighten it.

With the active Straighten tool, you can simply draw a line across the horizon. When not in view, you can draw a line that's indicated to represent the photo's horizontal axis.

After the photo has been straightened, the resulting edges will automatically be filled based on the option that you have selected.

You can manually straighten an image using the Expert mode.

In Expert mode, select the Straighten tool and then choose the option "Grow or shrink the canvas to fit your image."

The canvas can be used to fit the rotated image by resizing it. Straightening causes the corners to break off from the current canvas. The image also has areas of blank background, though no pixels are missing.

Crop to Remove Background

The straightened canvas retains the original size while also trimming some pixels.

You can use the cropping and straightening tools to remove the background from the canvas. The three different options are enabled if the Rotate All Layers option is enabled.

An improperly aligned horizon or horizontal line can be drawn parallel to the train. This can be done with the horizontal line drawn along the edge.

An improperly aligned horizontal line can also be drawn parallel to the vertical line. For instance, if the image of a tower is not aligned correctly, you can create a vertical line that's parallel to the tower.

Automatically Fill Empty Edges

The new version of the Straighten tool has an option that automatically fills the edges with relevant data. This feature is useful if you want to use the canvas without the background or transparent pixels.

Only the Original Size, Grow, and Shrink modes allow the Autofill edges option. Before you start drawing a line to straighten the image, select the Autofill option. When you draw the line, the gaps at the edges will automatically be filled.

In Quick mode, select the Straighten tool and then choose the option to maintain the canvas' size.

Maintain Canvas Size

With this feature, you can resize the image to remove any background that becomes visible after the canvas has been straightened.

Navigate to the "Straighten" option and choose "Modify." Doing so will allow you to alter the canvas' dimensions.

To align the horizontal line, draw it along the edge. For instance, you can use the image of a train with a misaligned horizon to show a horizontal line.

Draw a vertical line along the edge to align the image vertically. For instance, if your picture of the tower is not properly aligned, then draw a parallel line to it.

The automatic filling of gaps at the edges of the canvas is a feature that's featured in the latest version of the Straighten tool.

New in the Straighten tool is an automatic fill option that allows you to use relevant data instead of using transparent or background pixels.

Before you start drawing a line to straighten the image, select the Autofill option. This will automatically fill the gaps at the edges of the canvas.

Automatically straighten an image

To automatically remove the canvas from the image, go to the "Slick" option and choose "Rotate." The image has no background, although some areas have been filled in with blank background.

To apply the image's rotation and straighten it automatically, go to the "Rotate" option and choose

"Straighten and Crop." Notice that while the image doesn't have a blank background, some pixels have been clipped.

Divide a scanned image containing multiple photos

Scan multiple pictures in a single file and automatically split them into component photos. The photos must be separated to do this.

Scan images from a single page and create three separate images.

In the image section, choose the "divide scanned photos" option. In addition to automatically splitting the image, Photoshop Elements will also place the photos in separate folders.

The raw images are files that are created by the camera. You can choose to split the photos into folders or individual files.

A digital camera takes a picture using its sensor. Usually, the image is processed and compressed before it is transferred to the memory card. But, cameras can store photos raw, which means they do not have to do anything to them.

Rather than using the camera, you can open and process a raw file within Photoshop Elements. Doing so allows you to set the appropriate parameters such as white balance, contrast, and saturation.

To use raw files, choose the camera's default setting and save the files in its own format. When you open the files, they have various filename extensions such as NEF, CR2, and CRW. Only supported cameras can open these files in Photoshop Elements.

Although you can modify the raw file using the Camera Raw feature, Photoshop Elements doesn't save your alterations to the original version. After you have processed the raw image, you can open it in Photoshop Elements and save it as a supported version.

Process Versions

The Process Versions feature in Photoshop Elements helps you understand the raw file format. It allows you to work with the latest and greatest features of the format.

There are three Process Versions in the program, which are currently, two legacy, and one current.

The following versions are used for processing the raw image in Photoshop Elements: 2012 (default), 2010 (used in the Elements 10), 2003 (used in the Elements 9), and earlier.

If you open a raw image that has not been updated to the latest version of Photoshop Elements but was created using an older version, the current Process Version will be used.

To check if the current Process Version is applied to the raw image, go to the Camera Raw 9.1 dialog and click on the Calibration tab.

If the Process Version 2012 option is not selected, the icon located below the raw image will show that the older version is still being used.

Is it possible to switch between the Process Versions?

In the Camera Raw 9.1 dialogue box, click the "camera calibration" tab and select the "process version" you want to use.

The best version for you depends on the nature of your work and the requirements of your project.

Although the latest version of Photoshop Elements, Process Version 2012, is helpful when working with the latest raw files. But, if you have older versions of the program and your raw images are from previous releases, you can use the older version to update the newer ones. Doing so helps maintain the consistency of your older workflow and ensures that you have the latest version of the software.

The differences between the three process versions are significant.

The Basic tab in Process Version 2012 has the highlights, shadows, and whites sliders. In Process Version 2012 these replace the Fill light, Brightness, and Recovery sliders.

The Color detail slider has been added to the detail tab in Process Version 2012. It remains disabled until the modified version of this slider is available.

In Process Version 2012, there are two new features: the luminosity contrast and the luminosity detail sliders. These are disabled until the feature is modified.

Switching to an older version of Photoshop Elements will disable the newer sliders that are compatible with the latest version.

CHAPTER SEVEN

Camera Raw dialog box

In the detail or basic tab, click the "view options" button and select the "controls" section. You can also access various controls such as the RGB values, histogram, image settings, and the Zoom levels.

Navigate to the Edit workspace and choose the camera raw files you want to process. Then click the "Open" button.

The Camera Raw dialog box displays the current settings' histogram, which shows the variation in the image's tone. As you make adjustments, this feature will automatically update.

You can also use the various controls in the Camera Raw dialog box to change the way the image view is displayed. Some of these include the Zoom tool and options such as the highlights and shadows.

The preview feature in the Camera Raw dialog box allows you to preview the raw image with the settings that you have set. You can also choose to combine the settings with the hidden tabs.

To apply the settings that were used in the raw image that you have previously created, go to the Settings menu and select the "previous conversion" option. Doing so will help you quickly process the images that you have taken.

To rotate the image, click the "Rotate Image" button.

You can also set the white balance settings in the Camera Raw dialog box. This will help you maintain the ideal white balance for your photos.

In the white balance option section, you can also set the parameters that will be used to adjust the balance.

As you adjust the pixels in your photos using the Camera Raw dialog box, you can monitor the values of the RGB color space. Position your various tools, such as the Zoom, Hand, White Balance, and Crop tool, over the preview image to show the values of the RGB.

You can apply various tone adjustments to your photos using the exposure, contrast, saturation, and luminosity sliders.

To change the settings automatically, go to the Auto option and select the "undo manual adjustments" button. Then, select the "reset all options" option to restore the settings to their original state.

Follow these steps to apply various luminosity adjustments to your photos.

In Photoshop Elements, go to the "Open" button and choose the camera raw image that you want to process. You can then save and modify it in a format supported by Photoshop. The original raw file remains unchanged.

To stop the adjustments, click the Cancel option and close the dialog box. You can then save the changes in the DNG format.

Digital Negatives are proposed as the preferred format for storing camera raw files. These are useful when archiving photos because they contain the data from the sensor, such as the details about the image's appearance. You can store the settings in DNG files instead of using sidecar XMP or the camera raw database.

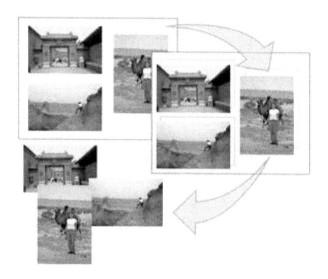

Adjust sharpness in camera raw files

The Sharpness slider can help you define the edges of your photos. It's a variation of the Unsharp Mask filter that Adobe Photoshop uses. This adjustment finds differences in the surrounding pixels and increases their contrast depending on the value that you specify.

The threshold that the camera raw plug in calculates when opening a file is based on the model, exposure compensation, and ISO. You can also choose whether to apply sharpening to previews or all images.

To get the best possible results, try to zoom in at least 100% on the preview image.

To change the settings automatically, go to the "Settings" section, click the "Detail," and then choose the "Sharpness" option. You can set the value of the slider to a lower one for cleaner images or increase it to the right.

If you're not planning on using Photoshop Elements to extensively change the image, you can use the camera raw sharpening slider. Turning off camera raw sharpening will automatically remove it from the list if you do intend on doing so. After all of your other resizing and editing activities have been completed, use the sharpening filters to finish the task.

You can reduce the noise in your camera raw images by using the Noise Reduction tool.

The Noise Reduction tool is part of the Camera Raw dialog box's Detail tab. It displays controls that help minimize the noise in your photos. The noise includes various visible artifacts, such as chroma and luminance, which degrade the quality of images.

To minimize the noise in grayscale images, move the luminosity smoothing slider to the right. Similarly, you can move the chroma noise reduction slider to the right.

When smoothing or reducing the luminosity or color noise, try to preview the entire image at 100% to get a better understanding of it.

Save changes to camera raw images

You can save your changes to a camera raw image by pressing the "Camera Raw" button in the dialog box. Although saving the file doesn't automatically open in Photoshop Elements, you can still use the "Open" command to open it.

To change one or more of the camera raw images, go to the dialog box and click on the "Save Image" button.

In the Save options dialog box, specify the directory where the file should be saved and the name of the file that you want to save.

To enhance the preview speed of the raw image, a small version of it is embedded in the DNG files.

This method adds a small amount of the raw image to the DNG file and makes the preview faster.

You can open and modify the raw image after you have processed it in the Camera Raw dialog.

The method known as lossy compression can reduce the size of your DNG files and cause them to lose quality. It's only recommended for raw images that are meant for archival use.

To store all of the original camera raw data in the DNG file, go to the "Save" option and click on the "Embedded Original Raw File" button.

After you've processed the raw image from the camera raw dialog, go to the Edit workspace and open it.

In the Camera Raw dialog, apply various adjustments to one or more of the raw images.

After the camera raw dialog has closed, click the Open button and the photo will open in the Edit workspace.

Settings and controls

Camera raw controls

Zoom tool.When you click on the preview image, the next value in the zoom range will be set automatically. You can also use the Zoom tool to zoom in on a specific area by dragging it into the preview image.

Hand tool

If the preview image has a zoom level greater than 100%, you can move it in the preview window using the Hand tool. To fit the image in the window, double-click the tool.

White Balance tool

To remove or change the colors of the entire image, click the neutral gray tone option. The values for the temperature and tint will change according to the adjustment.

Crop tool

Drag the tool into the preview image to remove a part of it. Then, click the Enter key to select the desired portion.

Straighten tool

The option to remove red eyes from photos of people and pets is in the Preferences section of the Camera Raw dialog. You can also set custom camera settings.

When you open a raw file containing information about the camera, Photoshop Elements will analyze the data to identify the model and set the appropriate settings. If you frequently make the same adjustments, you can modify the default settings of the camera. But, this doesn't work with other cameras of the same type.

To change the current settings, go to the settings section and click on the arrow next to the drop-down list.

You can use the camera's default settings in Photoshop Elements using the Reset Camera Raw option.

To remove the previous settings, go to the "Clear Imported Settings" option. You can add a variety of effects such as blurring, replacing colors, and cloning image regions.

In addition to adding a bit of color to your photos, you can also enhance them by using the Blur, Brush, and the Clone tools in Photoshop Elements. These tools can be used to replace the colors in the image or clone a part of it.

The Blur tool can soften the edges of an image by reducing the detail. It can also enhance the focus of your subject by blurring the background. You can use the Blur filters to achieve this effect.

The left and right photos show the effect of blurring the background. In expert mode, choose the Blur tool from the toolbox or press R to access the settings bar. The mode determines how the pixels in the image are blurred and how they are blended with the other ones.

From the menu item "brush pop-up," choose the type of tip you want. For more shapes, go to the drop-down list and select "brush thumbnail."

The size of the brush and the strength of the blur are set. You can also enter the amount of blur that will be applied using each stroke in the text box. If you want to apply all layers, select the option "sample all layers." Then, drag the part of the image that you want to blur into the frame.

The ability to replace specific colors in an image is simple with the Color Replacement tool. You can simply paint over a specific color, like yellow, with a different one, like red, in an image. In addition, you can use this tool to fix the colors.

To use the Color Replacement tool in expert mode, go to the Draw section and choose the Brush option from the menu. Then, choose the size of the brush that you want.

Tolerance can be specified with a low or high percentage to replace specific or diverse colors.

In Photoshop Mode, the blending mode is set to Color. You can also set limits by choosing one of the following options: discontiguous or congniguous. The former replaces the resulting colors wherever they occur while the latter is applied immediately under the highlighted area.

Drag the tool over the part of the background that's currently covered by the color to replace it.

To smoothen the edges of the area you want to correct, go to the Anti-aliasing option. You can also select the desired foreground color using the Eyedropper tool.

To set the color in the palette, go to the Tools section and choose the Color Picker. Then, drag the desired color over the part of the image you want to replace. You can also apply a clone to the affected area.

The image sample can be used with the Clone Stamp tool to duplicate or fix objects in your image. It can also be used to remove imperfections and add a bit of an image to another.

This image shows the original photo after adding starfish and then removing a character using the Clone Stamp tool.

In the Expert Mode, choose the Clone Stamp from the Enhance section, or click the S key.

Select the Clone Stamp in the Enhance section or press the S key. In the options bar, set the Brush option.

To set the tip of the brush, click the arrow next to the sample. You can then choose from the menu's category options and pick a brush thumbnail.

Sample All Layers

To copy and paste data from multiple layers, select the Sample All Layers option. You can also deselect the option to only sample the active layer.

Size

The size of the brush is set in pixels. You can set it by dragging the slider or entering the text box as the parameter.

The opacity of the paint that you apply can be set, allowing the pixels under the stroke to be visible. You can drag or enter a value to set it.

Mode

The blending mode determines how the pattern or source will blend with the existing pixels. In normal mode, new pixels will be added over the old ones.

Aligned

Even if you're repeatedly stopping and restarting the painting process, the sampled area can be moved with the cursor. If you want to remove unwanted elements, such as a rip in a scanned image, select the option to remove this from the list. If Aligned is not selected, the clone tool will apply the sample from the initial point. You can also select this option to apply multiple copies of the same image to different parts of it.

Navigate to the Clone Overlay option and set the following parameters.

Click the Clone Overlay option and choose the following parameters. Show Overlay will show the overlay within the brush size. Opacity will determine the opacity of the overlay. Clipped will enable the ability to clip it to the size of the brush.

You can hide the overlay while you're working on the paint strokes or invert it. Auto Hide is enabled when you want to hide the overlay completely. Invert is set when you want to change the colors in it.

To start a new sample, position the part of the image that you want to preview and click the Alt key. You'll then be able to copy and paste the pixels from the previous part of the image as you paint it.

You can use the tool to pick the desired effect by dragging or clicking it on the image. Alternatively, you can click and drag it on another target image. Unfortunately, the Photomerge Style Match is not supported in Photoshop Elements 13.

If you prefer an image's style, you can apply its attributes to another one. You can also work with a group of images and apply different styles to produce the best results.

The effect won't be cumulative if you apply multiple styles. Only the last one is saved.

After choosing the style of the image that you wish to apply, go to the Enhance menu and select the Photomerge option.

In the Style bin, add the selected images from your collection. Choose from pictures with strong stylistic elements and characteristics.

The Style bin displays the default images that you can select from.

Double-click the style image or drag it from the Style bin to the placeholder.

Use the various options in the Edit panel to refine the image.

Intensity

The intensity or amount of the style that you want to transfer is displayed. The maximum value indicates that you want to transfer all of the style.

Clarity

Enhance the contrast of a stylized image by adding more intensity to the slowly unfolding intensity clusters. This results in crisp details in the dark corners.

The details can enhance the global or overall contrast of the image. The Style Eraser can remove the applied style from certain areas. The Style Painter can add the same style back to the areas where it was previously applied.

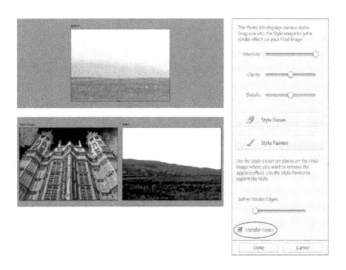

Transfer the style's tone to the other image in the collection. For instance, if the image you want to apply the Photomerge Style Transfer on is a colored one, select Transfer Tones.

Through Transfer Tones 5, the original color image can be changed to white and black. You can then update it with the new style by pressing Done.